ASK THIS!

Questions for Conversations

BRANDON W. G. WATERS

BALBOA.
PRESS
A DIVISION OF HAY HOUSE

Balboa Press books may be ordered through booksellers or by contacting:

Balboa Press
A Division of Hay House
1663 Liberty Drive
Bloomington, IN 47403
www.balboapress.com
1 (877) 407-4847

Because of the dynamic nature of the Internet, any web addresses or
links contained in this book may have changed since publication and
may no longer be valid. The views expressed in this work are solely those
of the author and do not necessarily reflect the views of the publisher,
and the publisher hereby disclaims any responsibility for them.

The author of this book does not dispense medical advice or prescribe the use
of any technique as a form of treatment for physical, emotional, or medical
problems without the advice of a physician, either directly or indirectly. The
intent of the author is only to offer information of a general nature to help
you in your quest for emotional and spiritual well-being. In the event you use
any of the information in this book for yourself, which is your constitutional
right, the author and the publisher assume no responsibility for your actions.

Any people depicted in stock imagery provided by Thinkstock are
models, and such images are being used for illustrative purposes only.
Certain stock imagery © Thinkstock.

Printed in the United States of America.

ISBN: 978-1-4525-9641-9 (sc)
ISBN: 978-1-4525-9642-6 (e)

Library of Congress Control Number: 2014907046

Balboa Press rev. date: 04/16/2014

1.   Do you work harder or smarter?

2.   Can a wood chuck, chuck wood?

3.   Could you change history?

4.   Is the grass really greener on the other side?

5.   Should the popular vote win?

6.   Does the President have enough time in office?

7.   Do we really have an Area 51?

8.   Who drank the half of the glass that is now only half full?

9. Would you be a policeman if you only ticketed stupid drivers?

10. What is the real reason gas prices fluctuate so much?

11. Is yesterday just a memory, and tomorrow is just a thought?

12. Can fools fall in love?

13. Why do people give their money to the casinos?

14. Is religion a business or a religion?

15. Should bowling be an Olympic sport?

16. Could a pot really call a kettle black?

17. Why do violent criminals get more than one strike?

18. Can money really buy freedom in a court of law?

19. Should marijuana be legal and alcohol be illegal?

20. Would freezing gas prices at 2 dollars a gallon stimulate the economy?

21. Is it kitty corner or kaddy corner?

22. How does a family of four make it on minimum wage?

23. Do you really think your daddy could kick their daddy's ass?

24. Does size matter go both ways?

25. Why doesn't grow cream make your hand bigger?

26. Do you think it could have been Adam and Eve &…Adam and Steve?

27. Why don't we drug test welfare recipients?

28. Can the mind heal the body?

29. How much more do actions speak louder than words?

30. Should you stay or should you go?

31. Does an apple ever fall far away from the tree?

32. Do you really think you can out run a helicopter?

33. Is it better to take a pre DUI or post DUI cab ride?

34. Would we cease to exist without daylight savings time?

35. How come sometimes, no DOES mean yes?

36. Did they tell you something you didn't want to know?

37.   Do we really know the long term affects from being tazed?

38.   Why are aliens green?

39.   Who is the fat lady?

40.   Does a raggedy ride, beat a dressed up walk?

41.   Where did on the lamb come from?

42.   Is seeing believing?

43.   Why can't supply meet demand?

44.   Why are yellow cabs white?

45. What if when we die our spirit is recycled into the sun?

46. Who said you can't?

47. How come nice guys, can't finish first?

48. Is reincarnation real?

49. Will pigs ever fly?

50. How can you be a juror if you do not speak English?

51. Can money buy love?

52. Is there life after death?

53.   Who said aint, aint a word?

54.   Is romance dead?

55.   Why do we exist?

56.   Does the person who dies with the most toys, win?

57.   Who said life was fair?

58.   Is there really a heaven and a hell?

59.   Do opposites attract?

60.   Can a polygraph be beat?

61. Why does your speedometer say 140mph, but you can only go 80mph?

62. How does someone get hit by a train?

63. If the oxygen is flowing why doesn't the bag inflate?

64. Why does it cost more to eat healthier?

65. What kind of person lives in this country, but doesn't speak English?

66. Wouldn't abortion be covered under our land of the free thing?

67. Isn't pro life just another way to say pro choice?

68.   Will we ever have flying cars?

69.   Why would you give your son a girl's name?

70.   Should you have to listen to dj's talk if it's commercial free radio?

71.   When is enough, enough?

72.   Why does sex sell?

73.   Are equal rights, really equal?

74.   Would prostitution be safer if it was legal?

75.   Is life, the answer?

76. Should professional athletes be paid so much money?

77. Do you let people know when they are doing a good job?

78. Are records meant to be broken?

79. Should it be harder to get married than divorced?

80. What if a welfare recipient had to take a parenting class first?

81. Won't we all eventually be the same color?

82. Why do we call brown people black?

83. How come we do not change things until a tragedy occurs?

84. If you have been lying do you say honestly first?

85. Will they do it for less money than you?

86. Is it the pit bull or the owner?

87. Why would someone stay in a miserable marriage?

88. How come you have to wear a seat belt but not a helmet?

89. Isn't an automobile, essentially a forward only, time machine?

90. Who is the greatest human being to date?

91. Are you slowly killing yourself?

92. When would you, compare apples to oranges?

93. Who bought the first pet rock?

94. If you don't make calls, can you make sales?

95. How could you hurt a child?

96. Why would you trap a man with a pregnancy?

97. Do the freaks really come out at night?

98. Can you really rob Peter to pay Paul?

99.   Does life exist on other planets?

100. Did we really land on the moon?

101. Did we really catch Osama?

102. Do you lie about reading the bible?

103. Why doesn't the media, focus more on the positives in our society?

104. How come one little piggy went to the market and the other one stayed home?

105. Would more people cheat, if they knew they could get away with it?

106.   What would you do if you were falsely accused of a crime?

107.   Is religion real or made up?

108.   Are you in love with your friends mate?

109.   Do you practice what you preach?

110.   Could you live without a cellular telephone?

111.   Can you love more than one person at the same time?

112.   Will a cheater ever stop cheating?

113.   Would you have done things different, if you could do it over?

114. Isn't your local power company a monopoly?

115. Do you say more than you feel or feel more than you say?

116. Could you transform yourself over night?

117. When does bad become good?

118. How long will you live?

119. Does it matter who does it?

120. Are you mad at yourself for getting rid of something?

121. Do you still write checks at the store?

122. Are puppies and kittens cuter than babies?

123. Is trying to do something any different than doing something?

124. Should you really live in this country if you don't think it's the greatest?

125. Why would you say one thing and do another?

126. Have you ever zigged when you clearly shoulda zagged?

127. If it aint broke, why would you fix it?

128. Are you fashionably late or just inconsiderate?

129. Do you really have, A best day ever?

130. Can you feel something wrong?

131. Are they all over the map?

132. How can we travel in outer space but can't cure cancer?

133. Does not inhaling really mean not smoking?

134. Will the east ever meet the west?

135. Is it just the dumb criminals that get caught?

136. Why are some things only 99.9% effective and not a 100%?

137. Wouldn't it be cool if more people owned submarines?

138.   Where did you go wrong?

139.   What was the point of that?

140.   Do you like them more than they like you?

141.   If twos company and threes a crowd, what's 4 and 5?

142.   Do they really want you to win when they wish you good luck?

143.   Why would you hug a person after they just knocked you out?

144.   Was their phone, really broken, that time?

145. Is constantly texting someone else while in the company of others, rude?

146. Would you trade your life for some other persons?

147. What's the best age to be?

148. Did you expect your life to be different?

149. Do you lie about the number of sexual encounters that you have had?

150. Are you jealous of other people?

151. Is there such a thing as love at first sight?

152. Have you ever been infatuated?

153. Can an allergic reaction just be in your head?

154. Was your college education worth the money it cost you?

155. Did you like or miss high school?

156. Would you travel back in time if you could?

157. Do you have a good relationship with your parents?

158. Did they make you feel one way, but they meant it in another way?

159. Are you unhappy now, that they live their life for you?

160. Is de javu real?

161. If you do the work, do you always get the reward?

162. Do things, really happen for a reason?

163. Have you accepted the things that you cannot change?

164. Why is telling someone to break a leg supposed to be good luck?

165. What's after video for communicating with others?

166. Is pimpin easy?

167. If you already shot the sheriff, then why not shoot the deputy?

168. Is coincidence ever explainable?

169. How much guessing takes place in medicine?

170. Have you ever said sorry when you really weren't?

171. Do you make your own luck?

172. Were you right, when you called it?

173. Was it the parent, or the kid, who invented allowance?

174. How much money would you have if you gave to everyone that asked?

175. If they told you, then you told others, how many people know?

176. Do you live to eat, or eat to live?

177. Would you run into a burning building to save someone?

178. Have you ever really, REALLY been in love?

179. If a fantasy could be your reality, what would it be?

180. Will a sexual disease stop you from having sex?

181. Is it okay to get a ticket in the mail if you run a red light?

182. Can a winner be a loser?

183. Are you a fan of public video surveillance?

184. Do you like yourself more than others like you?

185. Could you lead a double life?

186. When they told you, that you were wrong, did you believe them?

187. Why would you let someone ruin your day?

188. How many people do you really know?

189. Is sex, love?

190. If you both left at the same time, why did you get there so much faster?

191. Why did you believe them, when your intuition told you not to?

192. What made you think that person would actually pay you back?

193. Does goal setting work?

194. How many people have lived and died on this planet to date?

195. Do the good die young?

196.   Why is it still a secret if someone else knows?

197.   Will you be late to your own funeral?

198.   Is it their fault or yours?

199.   Could you ever lose something in your hand?

200.   Do you own a gun?

201.   Are you better then they are?

202.   Can you be beat?

203.   Would you win in a fight?

204.   Do you like your name?

205.   What do people think of you?

206.   Were dinosaurs, really here before humans?

207.   When do you tell someone, that you love them?

208.   Can you always, do it with a smile, if you don't enjoy it?

209.   Does what goes around, comes around, actually happen?

210.   Do you surround yourself with good people?

211.   Can you afford to buy it, if you can't pay cash?

212.   What would you change about yourself?

213.   Has infatuation caused you to make a bad decision?

214.   Is blood thicker than water?

215.   Would you blame someone else, for something you did?

216.   Are you a hypocritical racist?

217.   If you pledge your allegiance to someone, does it mean they own you?

218.   Do they say they'll call, but never do?

219.   Will you ever relocate for better weather?

220.   Can the littlest thing make you horny?

221. Why do you allow people in your life that constantly lie to you?

222. Is alcoholism a disease?

223. Does money excite you?

224. Will you ever try that again?

225. Who will we go to war with next?

226. Is it better to concede, if you know you can't win?

227. Why do you keep going back for more?

228. How many remotes do you have?

229. Do you let people know, that you feel, they treated you wrong?

230. Can someone be addicted to marijuana?

231. What do you think this country would be like without democracy?

232. Are you a name caller?

233. How do some people get through life?

234. When is it a good time to call it quits?

235. Have you ever fought the law and won?

236. Which is better, cats or dogs?

237.   Do street smarts beat book smarts?

238.   What the hell was that all about?

239.   How was, the west won?

240.   If nothings ever over till it's over, isn't it just over when it's over?

241.   What's the coolest thing you've ever seen?

242.   Is your life full of other people's drama?

243.   Do you really listen?

244.   Why is the relationship going to work this time?

245.   Are yawns contagious?

246.   Is forty the new thirty?

247.   Would you just stay at home with your knife during the gun fight?

248.   Do you say you'd donate a kidney, but you never would?

249.   Will you be buried or cremated?

250.   If you sell it will someone buy it?

251.   Do some things make you tick more than others?

252. Is doing what you love and loving what you do the same thing?

253. Do blondes really have more fun?

254. Does body hair grow faster the more you shave it?

255. Will mental telepathy ever be possible?

256. Are you a leader or a follower?

257. Would this country really be better with socialized medicine?

258. Couldn't the plan just be going with the flow?

259. Who flipped the first bird?

260. Is it humane to de-claw your cat?

261. Do more people regret or enjoy their tattoos to this day?

262. Is your TV big enough?

263. Do you know how to save money?

264. Can someone be right all the time?

265. Would you still eat meat, if animals could talk?

266. What if your mind wasn't safe from others reading it?

267. Do you look in the locker room?

268. Are you a talker or a doer?

269. If you were a beast, would a beauty want to be with you?

270. Which is better, sunset or sunrise?

271. Will you ever really know the truth?

272. Can you look someone in the eyes and still lie?

273. Was the past a simpler time?

274. Do you take a drug to cure an ailment that has crazy worse side effects?

275. How many grandmothers will we have with tramp stamp tattoos?

276. Do you choose based on what you think, rather than how you feel?

277. Is there a wrong time to voice your opinion?

278. Are kids growing up too fast today?

279. Do you constantly crave new information?

280. Could you imagine how crazy a sex change would be?

281. Have you wished for something that turned out bad when you got it?

282. Can people really communicate with the dead?

283. Would you have a pet if they could talk?

284. Why do the terrible twos last so long?

285. Do you tell them the truth, so they will be hurt?

286. Is cosmetic surgery really worth it?

287. Can bad things come in small packages?

288. Does your roommates' new mate drive you crazy?

289. Will that Jesus guy ever show his face again?

290. Is your God better than theirs?

291. Who concluded that one human year equaled seven dog years?

292. Have you ever anonymously paid for a family's dinner at a restaurant?

293. Why would you put the cart before the horse?

294. How do non profit organizations make it without profit?

295. Does fashion recycle itself every so many years?

296. Where would you rather live...past present or future?

297. Is that really your brain on drugs?

298. What's the most you can do without doing anything?

299. Do you THANK our veterans when meeting them?

300. Why is it easier to buy a private gun than one from a store?

301. When does a house become a home?

302. Are you okay to drive?

303. Does it just kind of seem like it's too good to be true?

304. Do you learn faster from self induced pain?

305. Is bald beautiful?

306. Can non fiction be fiction?

307. Could you do it for the money?

308. If you had to be blind or deaf which would you choose?

309. Would you falsely marry someone, so they could get citizenship?

310. Why do people travel to the Middle East?

311. Do you ever wonder what you see in the mirror?

312. Will you ever quit your bad habits?

313. Shouldn't all things, that are bad for you, be illegal?

314. When you need it, do you have it or have to get it?

315. Do you miss them more now that they're gone?

316. Would you rather drive, than be driven?

317. Will it be their place or yours?

318. Why can't you settle all debt for less than you owed?

319. Who's seen the most movies?

320. What's stopping you from starting?

321. Why can't tires last longer?

322. Can something resolve itself?

323. If someone has always been blind, what are their dreams like?

324. Do you loath someone?

325. Would you turn your best friend in for murder, if you knew they did it?

326. Do you trust easily?

327. Have you ever had your heart broken?

328. Could you sell someone out for less time?

329. Has your life ever been in constant danger?

330. Is it ever done, easier than said?

331. Are you nicer to the people that you want to have sex with?

332. Did a strip club screw up your relationship?

333. Do you doubt before trusting or trust before doubting?

334. Why should you have to push one for English?

335. If you flaunt it when you got it, what happens when you don't have it?

336. Is kissing sex?

337. Do you personally know any professional athletes?

338. Has the definition of stalking changed or what?

339. Do you want things that you don't need?

340. Will you do, what they tell you to do?

341. Who could lose twenty million dollars?

342. Have you ever been got?

343. How many people are studying our weaknesses?

344. Is lying cheating?

345. What really happened that night?

346. Did you lose your virginity with the right person?

347. Are you honest with people?

348. Have you ever lost because you beat yourself?

349. Does a wise man learn from his mistakes, or yours?

350. Is there a jack of all trades?

351. Would you do drugs if they weren't so easy to get?

352. Don't all the people in your family wear pants?

353. Can friends be lovers?

354. Why is it okay for some, but not for others?

355. Has your day ever worked out better than you planned?

356. If they have one, do you want one?

357. Does it make you feel inferior to ask a question?

358. Do they look like, what you thought they'd look like?

359. How deep is the ocean?

360. Do you think the sun recharges your body?

361. Would you want to hear someone's last words?

362. Were they really just friends?

363. Who do you love?

364. Can you live for free?

365. Is protesting productive?

366. Are Unions fair?

367. Are stereo types more true, than not?

368. What's your personal code of ethics?

369. If you already knew, then why did you do it?

370. Have you ever been paid to learn?

371. Could you walk everywhere?

372. Do the weak survive too?

373. Does the winner always deserve to win?

374. If it didn't matter if you won, then why would it matter how you played?

375. Can you persuade them to do it?

376. Should you do it their way, if your way is better?

377. Is the elder necessarily smarter?

378. Are you good at what you do?

379. Will you try it if you don't like it?

380. Are you a giver or a getter?

381. Does having a fancy car, make up for other inadequacies?

382. Who knows if animals really dream?

383. Could you be married to a porn star?

384. If you don't tell them, then how will they know?

385. Would you take money from a dumb ass?

386. How many times have they said they'd do something and never do?

387. When will they realize it's over?

388. Have you ever been told a lie, when you knew it was a lie?

389. Do you like to teach your lover things?

390. Is wrestling fake?

391. Will we ever be able to predict earthquakes?

392.   What would Earth be like without gravity?

393.   Are buyers liars?

394.   Can you get blood from a turnip?

395.   Could you eat someone else's words?

396.   Have people started a rumor about you?

397.   Is your life better, because you didn't do something?

398.   When can less be more?

399.   Did you ever lie, to save someone's feelings?

400. If you never try, how would you ever know?

401. How could there be proof in the pudding?

402. Are you with them because it's convenient?

403. Would you do it for free?

404. Can a genius be an idiot?

405. Why can't there be more internets?

406. Who is the luckiest person of all?

407. How come you can't wish for more wishes?

408. Are you too compliant, or should you be more?

409. Can you please yourself if needed?

410. Do you tell them what you think they want to hear?

411. Could you pretend to like someone?

412. Will they ever learn?

413. Is it true if you believe it in your own mind?

414. Would you go there if you had the chance?

415. Has being wrong ever been oh so right?

416. If there was no I in team, wouldn't there be no team in you?

417. Did you grow into your looks?

418. Is paper better than plastic?

419. Do you like to be alone?

420. Does everything happen for a reason?

421. Have you let life beat you down?

422. How could you talk to your mother with that mouth?

423. Do you want to, but never will?

424. Are you sure or just pretty sure?

425. Who will be left standing?

426. Does the truth, really set you free?

427. Do you have a poker face?

428. Why do people say oh instead of zero?

429. Is that color neon or florescent?

430. Could professional sports, be secretly scripted?

431. Will you drink tap water?

432. Would you do it if there was no possibility of going to jail?

433. If you were high when you did something, did it get done?

434. Can you cry on queue?

435. Who would know if probably cuts it more than not?

436. Have you ever planted a tree?

437. How much time, do you really think you'll need?

438. Are you addicted to TV?

439. Do you miss keys?

440. Does April Fools Day fool you?

441. Has anyone ever tricked you into doing something?

442. Is free always worth it?

443. Can you be fooled twice?

444. Would you be a vegetarian if you had to kill your own food?

445. How many questions do you really have, but never ask anyone?

446. Did you do it for love or the money?

447. Do you have a dream car?

448. Are you living at your means?

449. Have you ever lost on purpose?

450. Will a human being ever be cloned?

451. If the black box can survive the crash, then why can't the plane?

452. Why do you have cake, and not eat it?

453. Do you look to see if you're being followed?

454. Who's really the boss?

455. Would you be a doctor if your last name was Doctor?

456. What's the next best thing?

457. Do you believe in ghosts?

458. Are you secretly shallow?

459. Could you do better?

460. How would you feel, if you won the lottery?

461. Is caller ID better than sliced bread?

462. Do you wish you knew karate?

463. Have you ever gone to the store and bought nothing?

464. Does your family have a crest?

465. What if a bad guy wore white?

466. Has anyone, you've ever known, faked a heart attack?

467. Can you give a minor alcohol for a good reason?

468. Do you have a great idea for a movie?

469. Has someone taken credit for your great work?

470. Will people wait longer, if you're more important than they are?

471. Are there different definitions of entrapment?

472. Do you have jokes?

473. Why is the human body so fragile, yet, it can sustain so much?

474. Is crazy just an excuse?

475. Can you really say that with a straight face?

476. Does the valet snoop in your car?

477. Have you ever thought about framing someone?

478. What's the best brand of American automobiles?

479. Do they only call you when they need something?

480. Would you bend the rules for one person, but not for another?

481. Will there ever be another best TV offer?

482. Could hypothetical ever be true?

483. Are you a hater?

484. Do other people enjoy your company?

485. How much more successful could you be, if you never had to sleep?

486. Are you one thing, but people think you are another thing?

487. Can you do something that no one else can do?

488. What would the best of both worlds be like?

489. Does adrenalin, really give you unbelievable strength?

490. Do you believe everything you see on TV?

491. Would you do it again for the first time?

492. How can you know less now, than you used too?

493. Is your experience, their benefit?

494. Will there ever be enough time?

495. Who said cheaters never win?

496. What is taking so long to cure Alzheimer's?

497. Do you apologize, if you know you're not wrong?

498. Is reality television real?

499. Why can't the flag be red white and black?

500. Can it ever be done right, if you don't do it?

501. If you never vote, how can you complain?

502. Are black and white movies unacceptable now?

503. If you set something free, will it come back to you?

504. Do you keep a secret, if you say that you will?

505. Would you go into space?

506. Have you ever felt like you had a guardian angel?

507. Why couldn't the prison population be the country's farmers?

508. Is sex an international language?

509. Could your seat cushion be a flotation device and a parachute?

510. Has anyone ever told you that you look like someone else?

511. Have you ever strong armed someone?

512. Are you worth it?

513. Which television network is truly the best?

514. Why is the movie different than the book?

515. Do you help others without them asking?

516. Can someone truly be reformed?

517. Are you cool, or just think you're cool?

518. Would somebody save you?

519. Have you ever let someone down on purpose?

520. How could a robot be smarter than a human?

521. Where do all the people, who work in the Chinese restaurants, live?

522. Do you microwave your ice cream?

523. Should you have pets, if you're never home?

524. Who really keeps bones in their closet anymore?

525. Is your word, worth more than money?

526. Are they a perpetrator?

527. Who got the first early bird?

528. Does anyone, live at the dead end of a one way street?

529. If teachers made a lot more money, would the pupils learn more?

530. Do you ever wonder, what if?

531. Have video games changed children?

532. Has someone done something to you, out of spite?

533. Can silence be deafening?

534. Why would your heart be at home?

535. Does love prevail over sex?

536. How could someone live with cockroaches?

537. If there is video of you doing it, how can you say you didn't?

538. What do you care most about?

539. Have you ever been to a nudist camp?

540. What's really a girl's best friend?

541. Do you stand up for what you believe in?

542. Could their life be better, if they weren't so stubborn?

543. Will you do something new today?

544. Did you know someone who committed suicide?

545. Could a picture paint a thousand questions?

546. Do you go out of your way, to give a litterbug, their litter back?

547. How come it's Jerry that got rigged now?

548. Is a card game more luck or skill?

549. Where would you go without them?

550. Does someone owe everything to you but, will never admit it?

551. If you tried and tried again would you ever get it right?

552. Would you change your grandparents' diaper?

553. Could you put your parents in a nursing home?

554. Are you ever in it, to lose it?

555. Does the truth really set you free?

556. Is it easier to fall in or out of love?

557. Will you ever let that happen again?

558. How can a man get oral sex from another man and not be gay?

559. Why is the best, really yet to come?

560. Do you drink to get drunk?

561. Can you be rich without having any money?

562. If you took more time, could you do it better?

563. Do you like to take naps?

564. Would you go to a Physic?

565. Are you good with directions?

566. Will you go away if ignored?

567. Is any fast food good?

568. What's next?

569. Does the perfect specimen exist?

570. Did something extraordinary happen to you?

571. How can they do, what they do?

572. Why can't a car, get a hundred miles per gallon?

573. What would actually make the world better?

574. Do you leave you a voice mail, when you know they'll call right back?

575. Do they play too many commercials?

576. Are you tired of being over appreciated?

577. Is the journey so good, that you never want it to end?

578. Would your life be better, without them?

579. Do you like to touch things, before you buy them?

580. If you wait until you have enough money to have kids, will you ever?

581. Have you ever played hide and seek with adults?

582. Can you lye with dogs and come up without flees?

583. Is your motto: the hotter the person, the more you'll put up with?

584. Why would you have a pet, if it was a peeve?

585. Does dancing turn you on?

586. Do you like rap music now, but won't admit it?

587. If they say you can't do it, do you believe them?

588. Will it be a big surprise if you never hear from them again?

589. Could you have been adopted?

590. Have you ever cried to get your way?

591. Aren't the tough, already going?

592. How many computers do you have?

593. Do you wear hats?

594. Is Tuesday the most underrated day of the week?

595. Do they always screw you at the drive thru?

596. How can you win the lottery if you never buy a ticket?

597. Would you get involved, if you saw someone beating their children?

598. If it's the principle of it, then why don't you say something?

599. Can you get somewhere faster, if you go slower?

600. Are there times when you should keep your mouth shut?

601. Should they really be walking around without a helmet?

602. Would you drive if you weren't supposed to?

603. Does that mean all the other drunk drivers are better?

604. Have you ever had sex for money?

605. When was the last time something made you so excited?

606. Is it only as complicated as you make it?

607. How long would you wait for someone?

608. Would you open the door for a stranger?

609.   Do you still have a home phone?

610.   Why are supper and dinner the same thing?

611.   Were you born in a barn?

612.   Can doing something without permission, make it better?

613.   Should you be prepared for the unexpected?

614.   Do you know what a reticular activator is?

615.   If you write it down, is there a better chance that you won't forget it?

616.   Could you represent someone, even if you knew they were guilty?

617. Can your imagination take you there?

618. Could you make someone do something without them knowing?

619. Will your children really tell you?

620. Do you tint your car because you have curtains in your house?

621. How come the letter K is sometimes silent?

622. When will you think it's a good time to get a DNA test?

623. Are you just a good time?

624. Do you suffer from O.C.S, "Only Child Syndrome?"

625. Have you ever spied on someone?

626. Do you always do the same thing, if you always get the same result?

627. When did the definition of gay, change from happy?

628. Can animals fall in love with each other?

629. If Hell froze over, would it now be Hail?

630. Would you watch it, if you didn't like it?

631. Could somebody sell you something that you didn't need?

632. Do you remember all the phone numbers that are in your phone?

633. Have you ever been to a rodeo?

634. Did they just blow your mind?

635. Does a brown nose stink?

636. Are you a screamer?

637. If they build it, would you go?

638. Would you sell your soul to the devil?

639.   Why do we need F, if we can use P & H?

640.   Could a bad surprise, be good?

641.   Have you ever gone to the airport a day early?

642.   Do you correct people, who have bad English?

643.   Does practice always make perfect?

644.   Are things, supposed to be better than this for you?

645.   Was there really a frozen gerbil up there?

646.   Would you quit if you could?

647.   Can you fake it, till you make it?

648.   Do you try it before you buy it?

649.   Is quantity, better than quality?

650.   What will you tell them, if they ask?

651.   Has telling it like it is, ever got you in trouble?'

652.   Are you a good speller?

653.   Can you be saved from yourself?

654.   Would you eat less, if you had more to do?

655.   How much money do you really waste?

656. Are you out of your mind?

657. Will anything ever be the same again?

658. Do you step in other peoples dog crap?

659. How could they not have known, it was a man?

660. Have you let someone push your buttons, for the wrong reason?

661. Is mysterious sexy?

662. Would you do it, if you knew it was wrong?

663. Can love be intoxicating?

664. Why are some people so violent?

665. Could you do your job for free?

666. Will they call, if they say they are going to call?

667. Do you know roman numerals?

668. Why do you always make it about you?

669. Do they know that you know that they know?

670. Can you see the future?

671. Is there a best defense?

672.   Could you share a toothbrush with someone?

673.   Why is it harder to think positive, than it is to think negative?

674.   Do you tell people more than you should?

675.   Have you ever been afraid of your own shadow?

676.   Are you thankful, because you have it better than most?

677.   Why do some volunteers get paid?

678.   Could a lie have proof?

679.   Does music motivate you?

680. Would it kill you to try it?

681. Is it possible to live without mail?

682. Should Santa triple check his list?

683. Do you ever offer wrong advice, to get your way?

684. Are you a backseat driver?

685. Will you tell them, if they don't need to know?

686. If you blackout when you get drunk, then why do you drink?

687. Why do good things happen to bad people?

688.   Could boredom really kill you?

689.   Do you secretly make fun of people?

690.   Is it your fault that your parents are unhappy?

691.   Would you rather eat out, or cook at home?

692.   Do people that do not smoke marijuana have short term memory loss?

693.   Have you ever called a lover by the wrong name?

694.   Can something be over before it gets started?

695.   Could step children feel like your own?

696.   Are you star struck?

697.   Would you go, if they said they needed you to go?

698.   Do you share embarrassing stories about yourself?

699.   Will you have a good day today?

700.   Has a miracle ever happened to you?

701.   Are you convinced, your house is haunted?

702.   Could who you know, be better than what you know?

703.   How many true friends, can you say that you have?

704.   Do beautiful people make new friends easier?

705.   When you close your eyes what do you see?

706.   Do you keep talking when no one is listening?

707.   Have you ever set yourself up for failure?

708.   Why do you work at a job that you hate?

709.   Will you ever start or stop cheating on your taxes?

710.   Are you always the center of attention?

711.   Do you only wash your hands in the bathroom, in front of others?

712. Could there be a better way to do laundry?

713. Would you do it, just to prove a point?

714. Did you screw up the best thing that ever happened to you?

715. Can you ever do something for the first time again?

716. Do you believe that they believe it?

717. Why would you want to keep your enemies closer?

718. How could any time, be worth the crime?

719. If you ask, do you always receive?

720. Will the cows ever come home?

721. Can a quitter ever win?

722. Could you be easily replaced?

723. Are you always asking for forgiveness?

724. Why would you stay, when you know there will be trouble?

725. Would they be your friends, if they let you drive drunk?

726. Do you sing in the rain?

727. Are you a lover or a fighter?

728. Can you sleep, standing up?

729. Are you predictable?

730. Would you rather call the shots, or have the shots called?

731. Can you ever win from losing?

732. Is there a low way to Heaven?

733. Do you stop arguing, when you realize you can't win?

734. Should gas stations sell beer?

735. Would you ever be a ditch digger?

736. Do you accessorize?

737. Is make up sex better?

738. Could you travel for a living?

739. If you never try, will you be happy?

740. Have you ever risked everything and gained nothing?

741. Are you sure about that?

742. Can you get there on time if you leave late?

743. Does ground pepper really stop a leaking radiator?

744. Where's the bottle, it's all bottled up in?

745. Can you please everybody, all the time?

746. Do people really get married, to get divorced?

747. Could you tell a story with only questions?

748. Why can't you just start at the top?

749. Should it be beauty before age?

750. Will you quit before you start?

751. Do you play for keeps?

752. Are you afraid of what's to come?

753. Could you get a bigger bang for your buck?

754. How many different ways, can you ask the same question?

755. Can women cheat easier than men?

756. What is you favorite branch of the U. S. Military?

757. Is confessing your sins, just an excuse to sin?

758. Would you be sorry, if you woke them up?

759. Are you constantly accusing your mate of cheating, because you are?

760. Do you think they are giving you mixed signals?

761. Is your maiden name Swallows, and your married name Spits?

762. Do you start fights when you're out?

763. Can you judge a book by its cover?

764. What's the highest number that you have ever counted to?

765. Will your dreams ever come true?

766. Have you voted in every presidential election since you were able?

767. If you don't go towards the light will you survive?

768. Is there a wrong time to say yes?

769. Would you lose weight, if you ate less?

770. Could you do anything, if you just applied yourself?

771. Are scary movies stupid?

772. Did anyone fake their own death in 9/11?

773. How long is, long enough?

774. Do you know where anything will take you?

775.   Should someone you know be famous?

776.   Do you love to be loved?

777.   Are yawns contagious?

778.   Will your past ever come back to haunt you?

779.   Does playing dumb work for you?

780.   Have you ever been with a virgin?

781.   What will the next fad be?

782.   Has, what's your sign, ever worked as a pick
       up line for you?

783. Could there be a way without a will?

784. Did you ever think that you could get them?

785. Does anyone really know their own destiny?

786. Can a mistake be honest?

787. Are you misunderstood?

788. Could history be wrong?

789. Does alcohol make you promiscuous?

790. Have you ever failed miserably?

791. Do you like to shop?

792. Could you stop if you wanted to?

793. Can it still be true, if it seems too good to be true?

794. Is it all fun and games, until someone gets pregnant?

795. How many pairs of shoes do you have?

796. Are you the problem or the solution?

797. Has using a prescribed drug made your life better?

798. What's the best kept secret?

799. Were you trying to avoid those people?

800. Will they talk about you, behind your back?

801. Do you sleep naked?

802. Have you ever had sex with fruits or vegetables?

803. Are you a hustler?

804. Do you like to experiment?

805. Has anyone ever told you, to charge it to the game?

806. Should you have done it when you had the chance?

807. Do you do things before asking permission?

808. Do you whistle while you work?

809. Would you pick your dry cleaning up on a bike?

810. Is cheerleading, a sport?

811. How many steps, do you actually take, in a day?

812. Do you like the sound of your own voice?

813. Are more people, really behind on their mortgage, than we know?

814. Do you tell the truth, even if you know the result will be devastating?

815. Can there always a gray area?

816. When they're sayin it, do they not know they're sprayin it?

817. How fast does time really travel?

818. Do you pray for others?

819. Are others, prey for you?

820. Will thinking it, ever be able to make it happen?

821. Have you ever read a book, word for word, cover to cover?

822. Did you make up your own nickname?

823. What does, it's going swimmingly, mean?

824. Would your bail be denied?

825. Why would you straighten up and fly right, if you were really flying?

826. Who stuffs their pants with a sock, and expects good results?

827. Do you believe that if they're crying, they're lying?

828. Could you pull the plug?

829. Does it make you laugh, when people get hurt?

830. Would you make a good sketch artist?

831. How bored are your pets?

832. Would you drive a different car everyday, if you could?

833. Will you keep asking, until you get it?

834. Can you be bought?

835. Have you ever got lucky, from making an ass of yourself?

836. Are you relentless?

837. Do you like to make up new words?

838. Can you do a one handed hand stand?

839. Do you or someone you know, have incredible gifts?

840. Would you ever, offer yourself up, as a hostage?

841. How do you feel about time shares?

842. Do you lose more than you win?

843. Could you have done more?

844. Why do you mess with things that are going well?

845. Is teaching learning?

846. Are you always in control of your actions?

847. Who taught you how to tie your shoes?

848. Can you be hypnotized?

849. Do you have a fake fireplace?

850. Has wrong ever been really wrong?

851. Why is it a white lie?

852. How can they wear that, and not know?

853. Do you hunt?

854. Can it be real, if it is make believe?

855. Is anything sexual fun?

856. Why do they make you find it, instead of just telling you?

857. If you're sittin on 22's, should you be a drug dealer?

858. Would they rock your world?

859. Does the little guy have a chance?

860. Is a dreamer a schemer?

861. Have you ever let a friend, use your place to cheat on their mate?

862. Could you live in a house where the previous tenants were all murdered?

863. Who has all those statistics you're always hearing about?

864. How did they recover so quickly from that?

865. Are you a sucker for love?

866. What do you think about most?

867. Is it a lie, if you're the only one who knows the truth?

868. Do you laugh like other people?

869. Who determined the first tie?

870. When did stewardess, change to flight attendant?

871. Have you ever been in a snow ball fight?

872. Why don't you live, where you'd want to go on vacation?

873. Do you like politics?

874. Was slug bug, just an ingenious marketing strategy that stuck?

875. Have you ever been to a tea party?

876. Is everything a joke to you?

877. Can proper, ever be construed as improper?

878. Did you test drive one of those?

879. How could you know, they will make you happy forever?

880. Is there any reason not to call before showing up?

881. Do you look before you leap?

882. Would you tell people if you saw a bear wiping its ass with a rabbit?

883. Do you say that's funny, instead of laughing?

884. Can a nice steak on television, make you hungry?

885.   Are you in denial?

886.   Do you try and keep up with the world?

887.   How many times can you start from scratch?

888.   Was it fast, but worth it?

889.   Is it hard for you to fall asleep?

890.   What's your best memory?

891.   Would you be the good cop or the bad cop?

892.   Do you believe it, when people say, that you
       snore in your sleep?

893. When and where, will the first Michael Jackson sighting, occur?

894. Did you think for a while, that you had gotten away with it?

895. Are you easily beaten?

896. Would you do your job better for more money?

897. Do you exaggerate for effect?

898. Can a split personality be real?

899. Is it really out of your reach?

900. Will you ever do it, just to say you did it?

901. Does a pet make a better kid?

902. Have you ever been in love with a stripper?

903. Do you thrive, or choke under pressure?

904. What's the fastest you've ever driven your car?

905. Would it be you or them?

906. Could there be an alternate universe?

907. Can you believe that they didn't believe you?

908. Have you ever had to deliver bad news?

909. Do you have, a go to guy?

910. Are you really, ever satisfied?

911. Why would you want, everyday to be Christmas?

912. Will it ever, be your judgment day?

913. Do you know what portal to portal means?

914. If it smells bad, should you eat it?

915. Is it your convenience or theirs?

916. Can a song bring back a memory?

917. Why would you want to be built, like a brick shit house?

918. How many people can you really keep your eye on at once?

919. What are you going to do now?

920. Does so far ever feel so close?

921. Was it you fault they got hurt?

922. Could the push of one button, really kill us all?

923. Were you never there, but say that you were?

924. Would you sleep your way to the top?

925. Does anyone else know your secret codes?

926. Do you ever wonder if you chose the right profession?

927. Did all those people really have to die?

928. Can you start a fire with two sticks?

929. Who would you want to be stranded with on a desert island?

930. Have you ever lied under oath?

931. Why don't you teach your new dog old tricks?

932. Is your closet full of clothes that you never wear?

933. Would somebody, know you were guilty, just by looking at you?

934. Is a billion dollars the new million?

935. Are all massage parlors selling sex?

936. Isn't agreeing to disagree, an agreement?

937. Did it ever occur to you, that they might be telling the truth?

938. Will you stop before the job is done?

939. What's really behind those walls?

940. Do you live off of others people's money?

941. Don't they know you're lying if a little birdie told you?

942. Who do you know that has everything?

943. If it's out of sight, is it out of mind?

944. Would you save them, if you knew you would die?

945. Will you do it, if no one else will?

946. Has procrastination, ever saved you from something?

947. Is it wrong to look at other people, when you're in a relationship?

948. Does anyone know, the real you?

949. Have you ever been skinny dipping?

950. Do you always know where the exit is?

951. Could you decide someone's fate?

952. How fast is Godspeed?

953. Will we always be ushering in a new era?

954. Are you just waking up, or just going to bed?

955. Do you enjoy a good challenge?

956. Has pleading the fifth, ever work for you?

957. Is new, necessarily better?

958. Would anyone be interested in the book you would write?

959. Are you a racist?

960. Will they ever be on your level?

961. Do friends really have benefits?

962. Could a pill burn body fat?

963. Have you ever let something slip, that you weren't supposed to?

964. Has a friend of yours ever died from an overdose?

965. Do ya woulda, when ya shoulda?

966. Why would you want to be a fly on the wall?

967. Does anything go, all the time?

968. Do you talk to the TV?

969. How does one size fit all?

970. Can you shut someone out, without them knowing?

971. Do you always have to get your own way?

972. Will they have your back, if you need them?

973. Where's the craziest place you did it?

974. Can angels do it, while flying?

975. Is a million dollars, really enough for you?

976. Could there be a one man production?

977. Are you good at entertaining?

978. Does the first one to talk, always lose?

979. Would you live life different, if you knew when you'd die?

980. Do you enjoy the thrill of the chase, but always get the same result?

981.   Can you lose something in your hand?

982.   Is automatic, the new standard?

983.   Have you ever run out of gas, with money in your pocket?

984.   Do more people need to be led?

985.   Who thought they could do that, and not get caught?

986.   Are you surprised you made it this far?

987.   Did you put your hand down their pants?

988.   Do you buy things that you don't need?

989. Was the joke on you?

990. Does anyone, wish they were you?

991. Why are you so afraid to just ask?

992. Do you get bored easily?

993. Are there too many choices, or not enough?

994. Did you buy an expensive car, but can't afford to put gas in it?

995. What kind of questions, do you ask yourself?

996. Is sex with a millionaire, better than sex with the average Joe?

997.   Is it the penis or the vagina?

998.   If you don't know, do you pretend that you know?

999.   Have you ever talked to yourself in front of others?

1000. Could any of these questions, be your answer?

1001. Will you eat food past the expiration date?

1002. Do you rearrange your furniture regularly?

1003. Are you sure all your locks, are locked all the time?

1004. Can you always tell the difference?

1005. Would you like your car more, if it was a different color?

1006. Do you know what time you were born?

1007. Why do you do it, when you know they don't appreciate it?

1008. Is your past better than your present?

1009. Who's this nick that's always on time?

1010. Does everyone you know have good credit?

1011. Has road rage ever caught up to you?

1012. Why can't military time be the same as regular time?

1013. Can you see the picture in a picture?

1014. Have you ever lied on your resume?

1015. Who looks a gift horse in the mouth?

1016. If they didn't do it, then who did?

1017. Are you confused, or are they?

1018. Will you do it, even though they don't want you to?

1019. Would you be able to live your life on the run?

1020. When can the end be the beginning?

1021. Do you talk to your plants?

1022. Could there be a better way to get groceries?

1023. Was the lottery created just for suckers?

1024. Can you be nice to someone that you can't stand?

1025. Did they go one place, but told you another?

1026. What will the future really be like?

1027. Are you jealous of other people's success?

1028. Is your slang up to date?

1029. How many times can you watch the same thing?

1030. Do you investigate every alarm you hear?

1031. Would you really want someone else to wipe your own ass?

1032. Did that cause more harm than good?

1033. Is it harder to get started or finish?

1034. Does steady win the race?

1035. Why isn't 16, 18, & 21 just the same thing?

1036. Will you ever try that again?

1037. If you write it, will they read it?

1038. Do you say what they do?

1039. Would lying make you popular?

1040. When exactly, does close count?

1041. How could they think anyone would believe
that story?

1042. Who knew you did it and didn't tell?

1043. Is it better to get there first or last?

1044. Did your kid, kick their honor students' ass?

1045. What is the worst thing in the world?

1046. Can you find love in the wrong place?

1047. Do you look desperate?

1048. If it can't be done, why can someone do it?

1049. Would you go to a party where you didn't know anyone?

1050. Will you do it before they do?

1051. How did he, get her?

1052. Have you been hurt by someone you never thought would hurt you?

1053. Is checking someone out different than just looking at them?

1054. Why do you know that?

1055. Can something be proved without words or actions?

1056. Do you leave them always wanting more?

1057. Does anyone really have everything they want?

1058. Are you ahead of your time?

1059. Shouldn't it be a sticky dream?

1060. What's so good about a bad boy?

1061. Doesn't Celsius make more sense than Fahrenheit?

1062. Whose rectum got the first thermometer?

1063. Have you ever been cruelly humiliated?

1064. If you say you like them, then why would you bad mouth them?

1065. Can you have dollars if you don't have cents?

1066. Do people still go steady?

1067. Shouldn't you be able to see further away if you were far sighted?

1068. Does closure exist?

1069. Is it harder to start again the second time?

1070. Do you have an invention that could benefit mankind?

1071. Will you like it better if they do it?

1072. Were you raised with good morals?

1073. Are women crazier than men?

1074. Have you ever tried retail therapy?

1075. Can there be different definitions of dirty talk?

1076. Do you think you're fooling anyone?

1077. How do you say the word harassment?

1078. Who's going to take care of you when you need it?

1079. Is your life a lie?

1080. Are you a difference maker?

1081. Has someone ever taken your turn?

1082. Did that make any sense what so ever?

1083. Does it rain when it's pouring?

1084. Do their words differ from their actions?

1085. Are you always the last to know?

1086. Do you focus on one thing, when you should be focusing on another?

1087. Have you ever broken up with someone by text?

1088. Where else would you keep it?

1089. Could you really do that with a clear conscience?

1090. Did they deserve what they got?

1091. Are you afraid of your own success?

1092. Is global warming a scare tactic?

1093. How many automobiles have you owned at one time?

1094. Do you keep track of what you do for them?

1095. Can you see farther away than they can?

1096. Are their advances futile?

1097. Is the future predictable?

1098. Could that problem have been avoided?

1099. Was it all in your head?

1100. Did they do that on purpose?

1101. Do you always speak when you're spoken to?

1102. Why does the value of a dollar fluctuate so much?

1103. Is it a smaller world now?

1104. Can something be destroyed if it never existed?

1105. What good is it, if you never do anything with it?

1106. Would you be able to help someone commit suicide?

1107. Who knew what first?

1108. Are you always looking over your shoulder?

1109. Have you ever broken a promise?

1110. Did that really make you a better person?

1111. Would it make you weaker, if it didn't kill you?

1112. Was your answer wrong when you thought for sure it was right?

1113. If you dream it, can you do it?

1114. Would it be you or them?

1115. Have you already decided before they ask?

1116. Will it ever come true?

1117. When is the future now?

1118. What is a second world country?

1119. Have you ever lost a sure thing?

1120. Can any asshole do it the second time?

1121. Is the situation getting out of control?

1122. Are they growing more powerful everyday?

1123. Do you say anything just to get laid?

1124. Does your god talk to you?

1125. Will they ever grow up?

1126. Who can you trust?

1127. How can someone be thinking of nothing?

1128. Would you want somebody to do that to you?

1129. If you don't have problems, do you invent them?

1130. Is everyday a new adventure?

1131. Do you tell them, if their outfit makes them look fat?

1132. Why would you want to be on fire?

1133. What rules the world?

1134. Could you be a hired assassin?

1135. Did you have to walk to school, in the snow, with no shoes up a hill?

1136. Are you worth more dead than alive?

1137. When it doesn't look good, do you still do it?

1138. Can a woman take it like a man?

1139. Would you let someone have their way with you for a lot of money?

1140. Are you deep?

1141. How can you do that the rest of your life?

1142. If we are the United States, why are the laws different in each state?

1143. Is the answer a lie?

1144. Could things really be better in the morning?

1145. Is it one thing you did, or everything you did?

1146. Is your perception reality?

1147. Is your mind always working on it?

1148. Do you try to make other people jealous of you?

1149. Do you want more, the more you get?

1150. Is there a mother of all evils?

1151. Do you have some lies saved up?

1152. Can you fool yourself?

1153. Do you know that old saying?

1154. Did you ever hear that before?

1155. Do you have everything, but feel like you have nothing?

1156. Do you still get growing pains?

1157. Do you enjoy reading a good movie?

1158. Are you hard to stop?

1159. Have you written a letter that you've never sent?

1160. What is the essence of time?

1161. Has anyone hit the slot machine you just left?

1162. Were you a late bloomer?

1163. Did they go out of their way, not to tell someone, something they did?

1164. Does everyone know that you're their favorite?

1165. Do they want to, but you don't?

1166. Is it time to get started, or time to stop starting?

1167. Would you turn down a high five?

1168. What does the sign holder on the side of the road think about all day?

1169. Are you living on borrowed time?

1170. Do they really just drink in the closet?

1171. Could it still be true, if you were the only one to see it?

1172. When does it seem like the right time to do it?

1173. Will you share it before they ask?

1174. Can you get there without a plan?

1175. How is it, that everything is your fault?

1176. Why do you agree with them when you know their wrong?

1177. Who's working on the longer lasting batteries?

1178. Has their interference caused you headaches?

1179. Do you lead by example?

1180. Have you let them lead you astray?

1181. Will you pee in public?

1182. If you want to do it, do you?

1183. Is anything possible, unless you quit?

1184. Did you leave your last life behind?

1185. Are you creative or just confused?

1186. How far will you go?

1187. Have you been on the wrong side of the law?

1188. What do bugs think about you?

1189. Can you get stung on the phone?

1190. Would they have gotten away with it, if you did nothing?

1191. Is something desperately wrong?

1192. Do you know what's on every channel?

1193. Has time caught up to you?

1194. Why does being the president give you gray hair?

1195. Can you piss off the universe?

1196. Who takes a long walk off a short pier?

1197. Will you admit it if they have no proof?

1198. Did you get what you expected?

1199. Would you still take the high road if the low road was faster?

1200. Should there be cold cases?

1201. Have you called the police about a drunk driver?

1202. What would you take in a fire?

1203. Which way did they really go?

1204. Has a new friend ever done a background check on you first?

1205. If you quit, will they?

1206. Do you take the hotel bedspread off before you sit on the bed?

1207. How much time do you waste, watching television?

1208. Does your cell phone piss you off?

1209. What would you do if your plane was going down?

1210. Have you ever been paid for a visit?

1211. Did you do it because everyone else did?

1212. Where is the stat, on the stats?

1213. Were they just a victim of circumstance?

1214. Do you call trailers, wheel estate?

1215. Can you envision the completion, but can't figure out how to get started?

1216. Are their intensions genuine?

1217. Why would you beat around a bush?

1218. Is it time to change your look?

1219. Which one did you like more?

1220. If you fail, will someone else try?

1221. Will they do it for you, for free?

1222. Are you a creature of habit?

1223. Could your conscience stop you from doing something?

1224. How did they miss that?

1225. Did you play basketball with their check?

1226. Would you take them back if they promised to change?

1227. Were they served justice?

1228. What makes you smile?

1229. Do you answer private numbers or blocked calls?

1230. When you look at them, what do you see?

1231. When was the last time you mailed something?

1232. Who is your favorite person?

1233. What could you live without?

1234. Are you convinced?

1235. Can it be read if it's never been written?